The Piano Proficiency Exam Review Book

The Piano Proficiency Exam Review Book

Lucy Mauro and Scott Beard

OXFORD
UNIVERSITY PRESS

OXFORD
UNIVERSITY PRESS

Oxford University Press is a department of the University of Oxford. It furthers
the University's objective of excellence in research, scholarship, and education
by publishing worldwide. Oxford is a registered trade mark of Oxford University
Press in the UK and certain other countries.

Published in the United States of America by Oxford University Press
198 Madison Avenue, New York, NY 10016, United States of America.

CIP data is on file at the Library of Congress
ISBN 978–0–19–093393–7

9 8 7 6 5 4 3 2 1

Printed by Marquis, Canada

Photo credit: David Bess Photography, LLC

CONTENTS

PREFACE

To the student

Basic piano skills are an integral part of musicianship. Secondary piano studies in most college and university music programs are designed to help you achieve those skills, including technique, sight reading, harmonization, transposition, score reading, and solo playing. As a culmination of your keyboard studies, the piano proficiency exam allows you the opportunity to demonstrate the basic skills you have achieved. This book is designed to help you prepare for the exam, with a variety of music examples and exercises, concise explanations, practice suggestions, and self-tests. It is intended for use after completion of at least two semesters of class piano or one semester of private piano lessons and can be adapted to your institution's specific requirements. You will find more than forty standard melodies in this book that will build your repertoire of familiar songs. The book is also intended to be a comprehensive resource as you use the piano in a variety of current and future professional settings, including choral rehearsals, private lessons, music therapy sessions, and general music classes. We hope you find *The Piano Proficiency Exam Review Book* useful not only for meeting your school's exam requirements, but also in finding your own enjoyment in playing the piano and sharing music.

To the teacher

This book is designed to help students prepare for the piano proficiency exam, a standard requirement in most post-secondary music programs. Each review area can be adapted easily to your program's specific exam requirements. The book may be used in the applied lesson or as a primary or supplemental text for group piano classes, ideally in the third or fourth semesters of the typical four-semester group-piano curriculum or after one semester of private lessons. More than forty traditional songs are included to assist in building the student's repertoire of familiar melodies. The fingerings used throughout are designed for students with average-sized hands, with emphasis on standard fingerings that develop basic patterns and achieve keyboard movement with ease. We hope you find it complementary to your teaching and helpful in meeting the goals of your program's piano study and proficiency requirements.

Review I

Position at the Piano

The first important step in playing the piano is to use an appropriate seating position:

1. With the bench centered in the middle of the keyboard, sit on the first half of the bench with knees just under the keybed.
2. The bench height should allow your elbows to be level with or slightly above the white keys.
3. The right foot should be slightly ahead of the left, allowing for balance and ease of movement.
4. Sit up comfortably straight (not stiff or severely straight), with shoulders level and arms loose. Elbows and wrists should be flexible.
5. Stay in place on the bench and lean your body to the left or right as needed to play in the different registers of the keyboard.
6. Hands should be naturally rounded. You can find this position easily by allowing your hands to fall freely, with palms up, on your lap—then simply turn your hands over and place them on the keyboard.
7. Wrists should be level with the white keys.
8. Play on the pads of the first joints of the fingers, striving to keep the first joints from collapsing.
9. When using the damper pedal, keep the heel of your right foot on the floor and use your ankle to lift your foot. Depress the pedal with the ball of your foot and maintain contact with the pedal.
10. Use the same position for your left foot when you use the soft (*una corda*) pedal.

You should be able to demonstrate and articulate the proper seating, feet, arm, hand, and finger positions. The following photos illustrate proper positions with two students of different height.

**Examples of position
at the piano**

2

Hand and feet positions

Foot position on the damper pedal

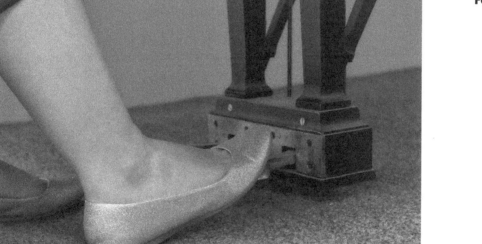

**Hand position on
the keyboard**

4

Review II

Scales and Arpeggios

Scales

Scales played with correct fingerings and good legato are at the foundation of piano skills. The first scale to become fluent with is the chromatic scale, which is easily played using the third finger on all black keys ascending and descending.

Mastering scales involves a clear understanding of the fingering patterns, and in particular, knowing when to cross over with fingers 3 and 4 and when to pass under with the thumb. Using visual cues such as arrows or circles helps to understand the fingering patterns. In the following examples, upward arrows indicate when to pass the thumb under. Downward arrows indicate crossing over with finger 3 or 4. Circles highlight fingerings that are the same in both hands and played simultaneously.

Arrows highlight fingers passing under and crossing over

Circles highlight the same fingering

The following fingering concepts are organized into groups to facilitate pattern recognition in your scale study. Ten scales have the same fingering:

Major: C, G, D, A, E
Harmonic Minor: C, G, D, A, E
- Third fingers play at the same time in both hands.
- Thumbs meet at the tonic at the start of the second octave.
- In the right hand descending, use the "3-4-3 rule": crossover first with 3, followed by 4, and then 3.
- The same crossovers occur in the left hand ascending (3-4-3).

F Major and F Harmonic Minor
- The left hand uses the same fingering as C Major.
- The right hand never uses the fifth finger.

B Major and B Harmonic Minor
- The right hand uses the same fingering as C Major.
- The left hand never uses the fifth finger.
- Thumbs play at the same time.

B♭, E♭, A♭, and D♭ (C♯) Major
- All use the same lefthand fingering: 321 4321

D♭ (C♯) and G♭ (F♯) Major and B♭ and E♭ Harmonic Minor
- Use fingers 2 and 3 on two black keys and fingers 2, 3, and 4 on three black keys.
- Thumbs play at the same time.

Practice Tips

✓ Check your seating position. Avoid sitting too closely (which restricts arm movement) or lapsing into slouching. Develop the habit of asking yourself before you begin to play:
- Am I at the proper distance, on the first half of the bench? Are my knees just under the keys?
- Am I sitting up straight with shoulders relaxed? Do my arms feel loose?
- Are my wrists level with the white keys?
- Are my feet slightly apart with the right foot ahead of the left?

✓ Use good legato, being careful not to overlap fingers or create gaps in the sound. Feel the fingers moving comfortably down to the keybed, "walking" smoothly from one note to the next.

✓ Use a crescendo ascending and a diminuendo descending to give shape and expression to your playing.

✓ Memorize the starting fingers for each scale.

✓ The most comfortable scales to play are B Major, D♭ Major, and G♭ Major, as they fit naturally under the hand with the longest fingers on the black keys. Start your practice with these scales.

✓ Play through a two-octave chromatic scale hands together once each day beginning with a different starting note.

✓ Use a metronome. Practice slowly with a starting tempo of ♩ = 40. Work toward a tempo of ♩ = 80 as a minimum goal.

✓ Include different articulations, dynamics, or rhythmic groupings (playing in triplets, for example) while using the metronome. These additions are helpful for building concentration, independence of the fingers, and tonal control.

✓ The start of the second octave is one of the places where fingering mistakes typically occur. Practice each scale hands together, but stop on the tonic at the second octave ascending, holding it for 4 counts as you think through the proper crossover. Do the same when you practice the scale descending. This exercise also helps to think of a two-octave scale as playing one octave and then simply repeating the correct fingering at the second octave.

✓ For extra help building coordination, "play" through the scales slowly, hands together, on the closed keyboard lid or a table top, reading the fingering carefully.

Major Scales

Write in your chosen visual cues.

C Major

G Major

D Major

A Major

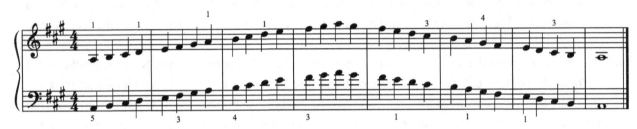

E Major

B Major

G♭ Major

D♭ Major

A♭ Major

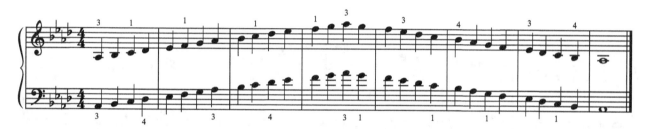

E♭ Major

B♭ Major

9

F Major

10

Harmonic Minor Scales

A Minor

E Minor

B Minor

F# Minor

C# Minor

G# Minor

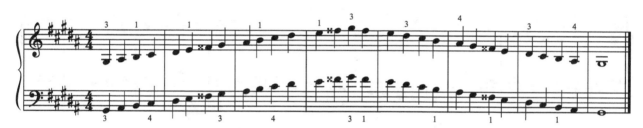

E♭ Minor

B♭ Minor

F Minor

C Minor

G Minor

D Minor

12

Arpeggios

Arpeggios are particularly useful for developing both a visual and tactile sense of the topography of the keyboard. An arpeggio is simply the notes of a broken chord played in succession. The arpeggios in this review are based only on major and minor triads.

An arpeggio based on a root-position triad and played hand over hand is one of the characteristic musical gestures on the piano:

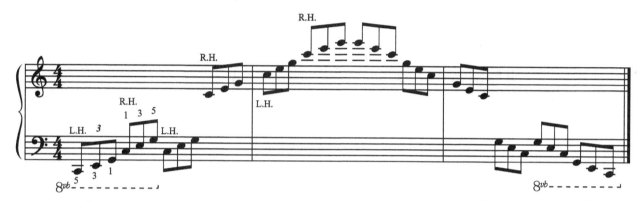

This arpeggio can be played in all major and minor keys using the same fingering and six-octave figuration. It can also be based on first-inversion and second-inversion triads using the following fingerings:

	Left Hand	Right Hand
Root Position	5 3 1	1 3 5
First Inversion	5 3 1	1 2 5
Second Inversion	5 2 1	1 3 5

Practice Tips

✓ Try sitting closely to the keyboard and play a hand-over-hand arpeggio; then move the bench to the proper distance with knees just under the keys, sitting on the first half of the bench. Play the arpeggio again. You will quickly notice the ease and freedom with which you can play when seated properly.

✓ Play through two different hand-over-hand arpeggios each day based on the root-position triad.

✓ Play through two different hand-over-hand arpeggios each day based on the first-inversion or second-inversion triad.

Major and minor arpeggios played either hands alone or with both hands in parallel motion use the following fingering concepts:

- *Right Hand*: All white-key major and minor arpeggios begin with finger 1 followed by fingers 2 and 3.

- *Left Hand*: All white-key major and minor arpeggios begin with finger 5 followed by 4 if there is only one white key between the bottom two notes. Finger 5 is followed by 3 if there are two white keys between the bottom two notes. For example:

C Major

B Major

- G♭ Major and E♭ Minor follow the white-key fingering rules noted previously. All other black-key arpeggios begin with either finger 2 or 3, and the thumb is used on white keys only.

Practice Tips

✓ Check your seating position. Is your bench centered in the middle of the keyboard? Are you at the correct distance and height, sitting up comfortably and straight? Stay in one place on the bench as your hands move up and down the keyboard, leaning your body as needed.

✓ Use good legato, being careful not to overlap fingers or leave gaps in the sound.

✓ Use a crescendo ascending and a diminuendo descending for shape and expression.

✓ Memorize the starting fingers of black-key majors and minors and other fingering concepts.

✓ Be careful to keep the wrist flexible but level as you pass the thumb under. Think of moving laterally across the keys without extra movements of your hand, arm, or elbow.

✓ Maintain the shape of your hand position as you move up and down the keyboard.

✓ Use a metronome to keep a steady beat. Work the tempo up to ♩ = 80 as a minimum tempo.

Major Arpeggios

C Major

G Major

D Major

A Major

E Major

B Major

G♭ Major

D♭ Major

16

Ab Major

17

Eb Major

Bb Major

F Major

Minor Arpeggios

A Minor

E Minor

B Minor

F# Minor

19

C# Minor

G# Minor

Eb Minor

Bb Minor

20

F Minor

C Minor

G Minor

D Minor

Review III

Cadences and Pedaling

Cadences built on the primary chords [I(i), IV(iv), and V7] are not only a foundation of piano technique, but also an integral part of harmonization skills. Cadences play an important role in defining phrase and periodic structure as well as the overall form of a composition. This review consists of cadences in root position, first inversion, and second inversion with progressions played in both hands and also in keyboard style. For the V7 chord, the 5th is omitted throughout for ease in hand position and development of piano technique.

When playing primary-chord cadences, there are two options for the fingering.

Option 1

- Places less emphasis on the weaker fourth fingers.
- Feels more comfortable for smaller and average-sized hands.
- Uses the standard fingerings for each position of the triad.
- Feels secure in the hands.
- Requires coordination for alternating fingers in the second inversion.
- Does not emphasize legato in the outer voices.

Option 2

- Feels more comfortable for larger hands.
- Emphasizes legato in the outer voices.
- Uses consecutive fingers.
- Places emphasis on the weaker fourth fingers.

22

It is important that you choose one set of fingerings and use those same fingerings for all major and minor keys.

Pedaling

Cadences may be played with or without the damper pedal. If you use the pedal, which adds warmth and color to the sound, listen carefully for clean pedal changes with each change of harmony. Using a syncopated pedal is recommended. This means adding the pedal off the beat as you hold the chord.

In the example below, the downward arrow represents pressing the pedal down. The upward arrow represents lifting the pedal. It is helpful to count as you pedal to coordinate it appropriately. Remember to keep your right heel on the floor and the ball of your foot always in contact with the pedal. Use your ankle to move your foot to depress and lift the pedal.

Generally, syncopated pedaling should be used when you see the traditional pedaling symbol:

As you practice these cadences, it is helpful to understand the half-step and whole-step movements of the voices.

Major Cadences—Half-Step (H.S.) and Whole-Step (W.S.) Movement

Root Position:

First Inversion:

Second Inversion:

Minor Cadences—Half-Step (H.S.) and Whole-Step (W.S.) Movement

Root Position:

First Inversion:

Second Inversion:

Practice Tips

✓ Check your seating position and remind yourself about all aspects of proper height, distance, and hand position.

✓ Listen to the quality of the sound. Use an *mf* dynamic in general.

✓ Add a crescendo or decrescendo as you play through the progression. This is a good exercise for developing listening skills and playing with tonal variety.

✓ Keep your wrists and arms flexible.

✓ Keep the rhythm steady, counting 2 beats between chord position changes.

✓ Think ahead. Look for the next position on the keyboard as you hold the last tonic chord.

✓ Practice hands alone at first to make sure you are using the correct fingering.

✓ Practice with and without pedal, both hands alone and hands together.

✓ Memorize the half-step and whole-step movements and say them aloud as you play.

✓ Focus on one chord as you play through the entire sequence. For example, the tonic chord is played three times in each position and the IV chord is played in second inversion, followed by root position, followed by first inversion.

✓ Focus on the resolution of the V7 chord in each position: The common tone is kept, the 3rd (leading tone) moves up to the tonic, and the chordal 7th moves down.

Major Cadences and Inversions

Write in your chosen fingerings.

C Major

G Major

D Major

A Major

E Major

B Major

G♭ Major

D♭ Major

A♭ Major

E♭ Major

B♭ Major

F Major

Minor Cadences and Inversions

Write in your chosen fingerings.

A Minor

E Minor

B Minor

F♯ Minor

C# Minor

G# Minor

Eb Minor

Bb Minor

F Minor

C Minor

G Minor

D Minor

The following progressions use the root-position cadence pattern in the right hand and the roots of the chords in the left hand. This is known as "keyboard style."

Major Cadences: Keyboard Style

Write in your chosen fingerings. The lefthand fingering should begin with 1 for all keys.

C Major   G Major

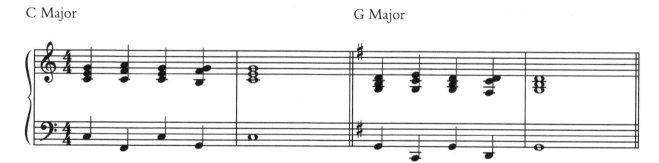

D Major

A Major

E Major

B Major

G♭ Major

D♭ Major

A♭ Major

E♭ Major

30

B♭ Major   F Major

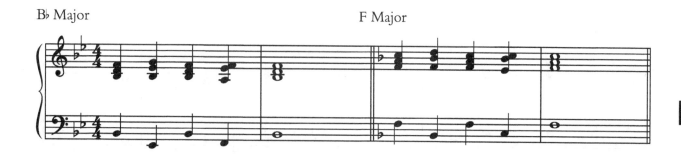

Minor Cadences: Keyboard Style

Write in your chosen fingerings. The lefthand fingering should begin with 1 for all keys.

A Minor   E Minor

B Minor   F♯ Minor

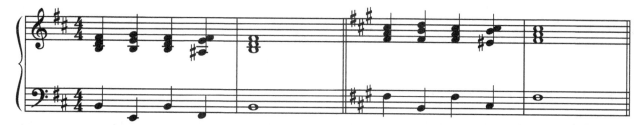

C♯ Minor   G♯ Minor

E♭ Minor   B♭ Minor

F Minor   C Minor

G Minor   D Minor

More Advanced Progressions

The following progressions use traditional chord movements and are helpful in preparing for harmonizations that move beyond primary chords. Practice transposing these progressions to all major and minor keys as appropriate.

Left hand only with typical cadential use of the ii chord:

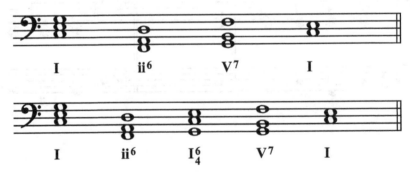

I   ii⁶   V⁷   I

I   ii⁶   I⁶₄   V⁷   I

Keyboard style with primary and secondary chords and secondary dominants:

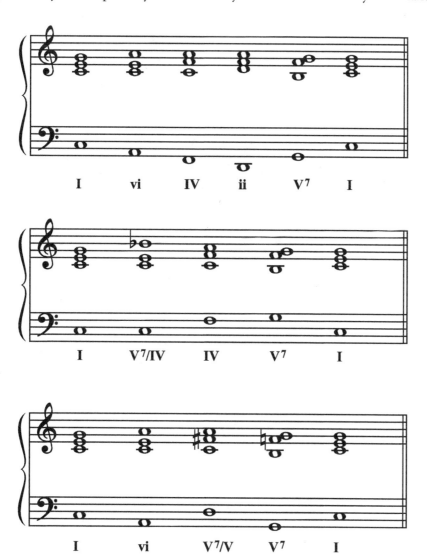

Review IV

Vocal Warm-Up Exercises

This review includes a variety of examples for accompanying and leading vocal warm-ups. These exercises, which are useful for both the rehearsal hall and the private studio, are based on chord progressions and melodic patterns played chromatically. For ease in reading, all chromatic examples are presented using flat-key signatures. In each example, write in your chosen fingerings based on the cadence patterns in the previous review. You should be able to play and sing at least two of these examples from memory. See the practice tips for suggested syllables and other helpful information.

Playing a simple single-chord accompaniment or a five-finger pattern chromatically, as in the three examples below, is an effective way to begin.

Vocal Warm-Up Exercise 1

Variations:

1. Substitute scale degree 5 on beat 2 in the left hand.
2. Play in minor.
3. Change the second chord in the right hand to IV6/4 in major and iv 6/4 in minor.

Continue the pattern chromatically ascending and descending.

Vocal Warm-Up Exercise 2

Continue the pattern chromatically ascending and descending.

Vocal Warm-Up Exercise 3

Continue the pattern chromatically ascending and descending.

The following vocal warm-ups use alternating-hand accompaniment patterns.

Vocal Warm-Up Exercise 4 in Major

38

Vocal Warm-Up Exercise 5 in Major

39

40

Vocal Warm-Up Exercise 6 in Minor

For the following vocal warm-up exercises, the accompaniments may be based on the previous examples. Continue the patterns chromatically.

Vocal Warm-Up Exercise 7:

Continue the pattern descending. Use the accompaniment pattern from Warm-Up Exercise 1 or 2.

Vocal Warm-Up Exercise 8

Continue the pattern ascending. Use an alternating-hand accompaniment pattern.

Vocal Warm-Up Exercise 9

Continue the pattern ascending. Use an alternating-hand accompaniment pattern.

Vocal Warm-Up Exercise 10

Excerpt from *An Hour of Study* by Pauline Viardot (1821–1910).

44

Practice Tips

✓ Check your seating position. Are you sitting up straight? Good posture and energy are essential when leading vocal warm-ups.

✓ Practice playing five-finger patterns and chord progressions chromatically in major and minor, starting from any key, ascending and descending.

✓ Use the metronome to keep a steady beat. Work up to a typical tempo of ♩ = 120, but be able to play these warm-ups at a variety of slower and faster speeds.

✓ Sing the vocal line while you play. Typical syllables to use are *me, may, mah, moh,* or *moo*. Vary the vocal lines by using different syllables, vowels, or words.

✓ Use an *mf* or *f* dynamic.

✓ If using the damper pedal, be careful to change the pedal with each chord change. Listen carefully and avoid pedal blurs.

✓ When adding the German +6 chord in Vocal Warm-Up 4, keep in mind it is also the dominant seventh from the successive key.

✓ Experiment with different accompanying patterns.

✓ Play the vocal line in the right hand and the chords in the left hand.

✓ Incorporate conducting as you play the accompaniments, using the pedal as needed to hold the longer notes and one hand to gesture. Modify the accompaniments to play with one hand as appropriate.

Review V

Harmonization and Transposition

The familiar tunes included in this review are useful in a variety of social, educational, and professional situations. You should be able to harmonize these simple songs either by playing the melody in your right hand with the chords in your left hand or in a keyboard style with the accompaniment distributed between the hands.

The root-position cadence pattern is one of the easiest and most effective ways to harmonize simple melodies. This position is also the basis for harmonizations that include secondary diatonic chords and chromatic harmonies, keeping the common tones as much as possible and moving easily to the nearest chord tones. For some harmonizations, however, it may be necessary to shift the hand entirely to move to a new chord. Often this provides a more stable sense of harmony.

For basic harmonizations, the accompaniment pattern should be consistent throughout a piece. Choose an accompaniment pattern that matches the character of the melody and keeps the pulse clear. Use simple rhythmic figures, especially if the melody has an active rhythmic motion.

Accompanying Patterns

The following examples of lefthand harmonization accompanying patterns are based on blocked and broken chords:

Blocked chord:

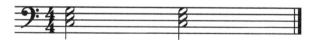

Broken chord:

Broken chord:

Broken chord:

Alberti bass:

Arpeggiated:

Western style:

The following examples are in keyboard style using both hands.

Alternating left and right hands:

Waltz style:

Broken chord:

Blues style:

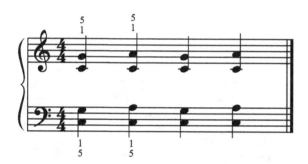

Adding an introduction and ending enhances a harmonization and helps to communicate character and interest. Arpeggios are useful for this along with simple dominant-tonic pitches played in contrasting registers:

In the example below, "Happy Birthday," the introduction uses the starting pitch of the melody. The harmonization and ending are based on a root-position cadence pattern and arpeggio.

Happy Birthday   Traditional/Patty Hill (1868–1946) and Mildred Hill (1859–1916)

Practice Tips—Harmonization

✓ Check your seating position. Are there issues you need to address such as slouching, sitting too closely, or keeping your wrists level with the white keys?

✓ Use the root-position cadence pattern as the basis for your harmonizations.

✓ When using the root-position V7 to I or i progression, the tonic chord typically needs only two notes (the root and 3rd) for proper voice leading (resolving the 3rd up and chordal 7th down).

✓ Keep the harmonization rhythm consistent (for example, using half-note chords throughout in 4/4 or an ascending quarter-note pattern in 3/4).

✓ If adding an introduction or ending, keep them rhythmic and in the same meter and tempo.

✓ Avoid leaving rhythmic gaps in the harmonization. For example, if the melody uses long note values or rests, use a half-note or quarter-note rhythm to highlight the rhythmic motion.

✓ If using pedal, do so sparingly, being careful to change with the harmonic and melodic movement.

✓ When playing the melody in the right hand and the accompaniment in the left, the hands may briefly overlap. Keep the fingers relaxed and flexible as they share the same key. To avoid overlapping, the melody may be played an octave higher or the accompaniment an octave lower for the entire song or for phrases that overlap.

Practice Tips—Transposition

✓ Write the harmonic analysis in Roman numerals in each example for ease of transposing.

✓ Transpose each melody to close and distant keys. For keys up to a 3rd apart, it is often easier to transpose "vertically," reading above or below the given note. For keys farther away (a 4th or more), reading intervals "horizontally" from note to note is typically easier.

✓ Be consistent when transposing, reading horizontally (following the intervals of the melodic line) or vertically (reading directly above or below the given note). To avoid confusion, do not combine the two methods.

...onization and Transposition Repertoire

...uette

Home on the Range

Daniel E. Kelley (1843–1905)

50

The Farmer in the Dell

Traditional

For He's a Jolly Good Fellow

Traditional

Hush Little Baby

Traditional

My Bonnie Lies Over the Ocean

Traditional

52

I've Been Workin' on the Railroad

Erie Canal

Thomas S. Allen (1876–1919)

Danny Boy (Londonderry Air)

Traditional

Beautiful Dreamer

Stephen Foster (1826–1864)

Take Me Out to the Ball Game

Albert von Tilzer (1878–1956)

Dona Nobis Pacem

Traditional

Excerpt from Symphony No. 9 ("Ode to Joy")

Ludwig van Beethoven (1770–1827)

Amazing Grace

Funiculì, Funiculà

Luigi Denza (1846–1922)

Auld Lang Syne

Jingle Bells

James Lord Pierpont (1822–1893)

61

Go Tell It On the Mountain

Spiritual

What Child Is This? (Greensleeves)

Traditional

62

How Great Thou Art

Traditional

Hark! The Herald Angels Sing

Felix Mendelssohn (1809–1847)

Joy to the World

George Frideric Handel (1685–1759)

64

Excerpt from Pomp and Circumstance, Op. 39, No. 1

Edward Elgar (1857–1934)

America the Beautiful

Samuel A. Ward (1847–1903)

65

America (My Country, 'Tis of Thee)

Traditional/arr. Thomas Arne (1710–1778)

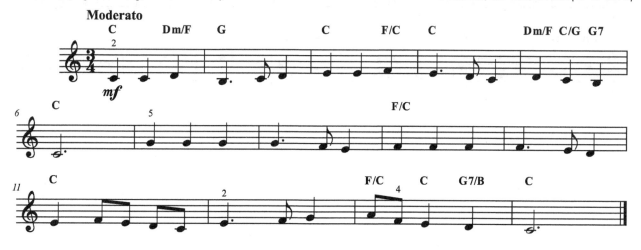

The Star-Spangled Banner

John Stafford Smith (1750–1836)

Review VI

Sight Reading

Sight reading, or the ability to play a piece without previous preparation, is a skill that enhances overall musicianship. Improving this skill requires devoting time each day to playing through a few measures of new music at or below your current level of study. Sight reading is an opportunity to synthesize your keyboard abilities with your understanding of harmony, melody, rhythm, and form. The examples in this review use many of the foundational figures you have been studying.

Practice Tips

- ✓ Check your seating position. Students often want to sit too close to the keyboard when reading an unfamiliar piece. Make sure to begin with the proper seating position and maintain it.
- ✓ Sight read for five to ten minutes each day, setting aside a time separate from your practice sessions.
- ✓ Look over the piece thoroughly before you begin to play, checking the key, tempo, dynamics, accidentals, and harmonic and melodic patterns.
- ✓ Make sure you are in the correct octaves on the keyboard by relating the first notes on the staff to middle C.
- ✓ Read up from the bottom staff. It is common to focus only on the treble line and ignore the bass. Patiently read the lower staff first when playing hands together.
- ✓ Sight read at a slow tempo and keep a steady beat. Count out loud, but avoid singing the counting along with the melodic line. Speak your counting strongly and securely with your hands following your counting.
- ✓ Sight read hands together. If it is necessary to read hands alone, begin with the most difficult line first.
- ✓ Keep your eyes on the page and allow your fingers to find the correct notes. Look at the keyboard only for the starting position and any large leaps.

Sight-Reading Repertoire

Andante

Scott Beard (b. 1964)

68

First Term at the Piano, Sz. 53, No. 2

Béla Bartók (1881–1945)

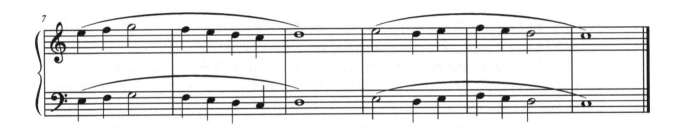

Moderato

Scott Beard (b. 1964)

Allegretto

Scott Beard (b. 1964)

First Term at the Piano, Sz. 53, No. 5

Béla Bartók (1881–1945)

Merrily We Roll Along

Traditional/Arr. Scott Beard (b. 1964)

70

First Term at the Piano, Sz. 53, No. 7

Béla Bartók (1881–1945)

Lento assai

Scott Beard (b. 1964)

Excerpt from *First Term at the Piano*, Sz. 53, No. 8

Béla Bartók (1881–1945)

Andante

Scott Beard (b. 1964)

72

Excerpt from *12 Easy Studies*, Op. 157, No. 1

Louis Köhler (1820–1886)

Excerpt from *Menuet en Rondeau*

Jean-Philippe Rameau (1683–1764)

St. Flavian (Hymn)

16th century/arr. Scott Beard (b. 1964)

Lightly Row

Traditional/arr. Scott Beard (b. 1964)

74

Excerpt from *Sight Reading Exercises*, Op. 45, No. 25

Arnoldo Sartorio (1853–1936)

Allegretto

Scott Beard (b. 1964)

***Sight Reading Exercises*, Op. 45, No. 25**

Arnoldo Sartorio (1853–1936)

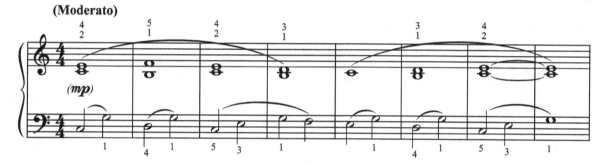

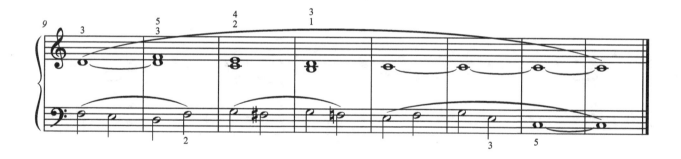

Excerpt from Minuet

Georg Telemann (1681–1767)

76

Excerpt from *Sight Reading Exercises*, Op. 45, No. 40

Arnoldo Sartorio (1853–1936)

Sight Reading Exercises, Op. 45, No. 31

Arnoldo Sartorio (1853–1936)

77

Burleske

Leopold Mozart (1719–1787)

D.C. sin al fine

Alla tedesca

Scott Beard (b. 1964)

Excerpt from *First Term at the Piano*, Sz. 53, No. 15

Béla Bartók (1881–1945)

Excerpt from *First Term at the Piano*, Sz. 53, No. 21

Béla Bartók (1881–1945)

Prelude No. 4 from *12 Short Pieces*

Henri Bertini (1798–1876)

Excerpt from *La Candeur*, Op. 100, No. 1

Johann Friedrich Burgmüller (1806–1874)

100 Progressive Studies, Op. 139, No. 7

Carl Czerny (1791–1857)

81

Excerpt from Prelude (Night) from *In the Bottoms*

R. Nathaniel Dett (1882–1943)

82

Excerpt from *An Hour of Study*

Pauline Viardot (1821–1910)

Excerpt from *Le Courant Limpide*, Op. 100, No. 1

J. Friedrich Burgmüller (1806–1874)

Sight Reading Exercises, Op. 45, No. 35

Arnoldo Sartorio (1853–1936)

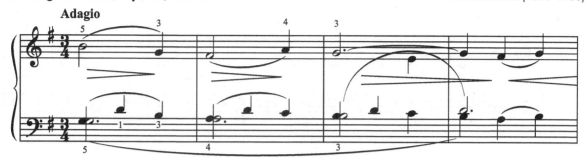

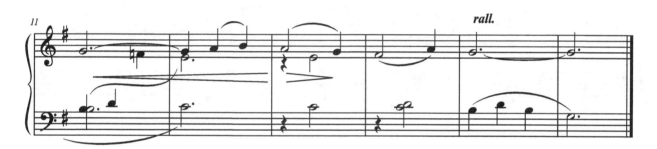

From *Easy Preludes for Students*

Clara Schumann (1819–1896)

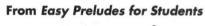

Prelude No. 10 from *12 Short Pieces*

Henri Bertini (1798–1876)

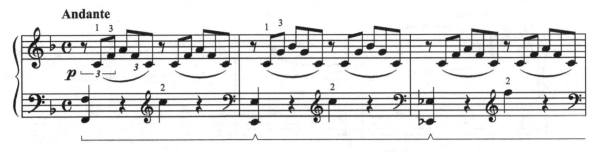

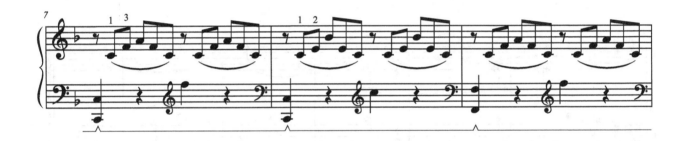

Ländler

Franz Schubert (1797–1828)

Excerpt from *La Farfalletta*

Vincenzo Bellini (1801–1835)

Andantino

Far - fal - let - ta, a - spet - ta a spet - ta; non vo -

88

lar con tan - ta fret - ta. Far del mal non ti vo -

gl'i - o; Fer - ma ap - pa - ga il de - sir— mi - o.

Excerpt from _Vaga luna, che inargenti_

Vincenzo Bellini (1801–1835)

89

Excerpt from *Nina*

Giovanni Battista Pergolesi (1710–1736)

Tre —— gior - ni son che Ni - na, che

Ni - na, che Ni - na in le - tto se ne

sta, —————————— in — le - tto —— se ne sta.

90

Excerpt from Sonata for Piano and Cello, Op. 11

Hélène Liebmann (1796—after 1835)

Excerpt from *Cantique*

Nadia Boulanger (1887–1979)

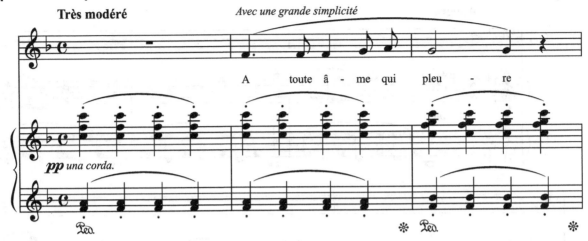

A toute â - me qui pleu — re

A tout pé - ché qui pas - se   J'ouvre au sein des é - toi - les Mes

Excerpt from *An Die Musik*, D. 547

Franz Schubert (1797–1828)

Review VII

Improvisation

Improvisation at the keyboard has a long and varied history, from being a required skill in the seventeenth and eighteenth centuries to today's most prominent use in jazz performance. The ability to create music spontaneously is a valued skill with relevance for musicians in a variety of settings. It is an especially useful skill for classroom teachers and music therapists. Improvisation requires strong rhythmic skills, an understanding of harmonic movement and melodic shape, and the ability to use standard pianistic figures and different registers of the keyboard with ease.

One of the best ways to begin improvising is to practice variations on patterns you already know, such as scales, cadences, and arpeggios. Methodically adding one new element at a time, such as a rolled chord, a nonchord tone, or a register change, helps to focus your musical intention, develop fluency, and build a repertoire of musical gestures. Embellishing familiar melodic and harmonic figures (and transposing them to different keys) is a good way to gain confidence and skill in improvisation. Another helpful guideline is to use repetition. Instead of trying to make each phrase unique, repeat what you know and can do well, incorporating repetition into the structure of your improvisation; then, try changing the motive slightly as you develop your piece. By using some basic parameters, you will gradually develop the freedom to improvise comfortably at the keyboard.

Carl Czerny (1791–1857) and Philip Antony Corri (1784–1832) each wrote method books for developing keyboard improvisational skills. These books were centered on "preluding," which was the tradition of playing a short improvisation as a preparation or introduction before the performance of a piece. In his *Original System of Preluding*, Corri begins by arpeggiating traditional chord progressions. The following two exercises are adapted from Corri's examples and should be practiced in all major and minor keys:

The next two examples by Corri use major scales. Practice each in all major and minor keys. Notice the different registers for the final tonic notes in the left hand.

1st Coda in A Major   P. A. Corri (1784–1832)

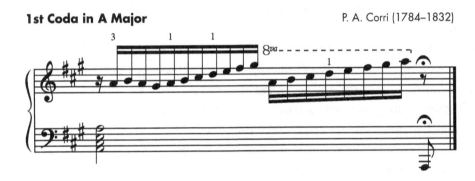

2nd Coda in A Major   P. A. Corri (1784–1832)

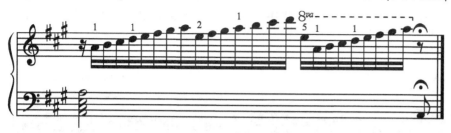

As preparation for the next exercise by Corri, use the third finger of the right hand to play through an arpeggiated root position major triad:

Add a half-step grace note with finger 2:

In a triplet rhythm, add one additional note and pass the thumb under for Corri's exercise:

5th Prelude in G Major   P. A. Corri (1784–1832)

Similar to the Prelude in G, begin this exercise by playing through the ascending C Major triad with finger 3 in the right hand. Follow all fingerings, being careful to pass the thumb under smoothly.

Excerpt from 5th Prelude in C Major   P. A. Corri (1784–1832)

98

The next exercise uses rolled chords. To roll the chord, play each note in succession, starting with the lowest note.

Excerpt from 5th Prelude in C Major   P. A. Corri (1784–1832)

Combine the rolled-chord cadence with the embellished triad outlined in the right hand:

5th Prelude in C Major   P. A. Corri (1784–1832)

Practice improvising on a root position cadence pattern, with one nonchord tone added. For example:

Using a familiar bass line, such as the ground bass from "Canon in D" by Johann Pachelbel (1653–1706), improvise a melody using only chord tones in the right hand, being careful with the voice leading and melodic shape:

Add passing tones:

In "Mary Had A Little Lamb," "Twinkle, Twinkle Little Star," and "When The Saints Go Marching In," improvise using the following:

1. Passing tones and other nonchord tones.
2. Grace notes (playing half or whole steps almost simultaneously with the main notes).
3. Different registers of the keyboard.
4. Mode change to the parallel minor.
5. An introduction and an ending based on the above examples by Corri.
6. Transposition to other keys.
7. Different accompaniment patterns. Use the lefthand patterns found in Review V as a basis.

Mary Had A Little Lamb

Lowell Mason (1792–1872)

100

Twinkle, Twinkle Little Star

Traditional

When The Saints Go Marching In

Improvise on the following progression using the 7th-chord pattern as a basis and methodically incorporate the following:

1. Rolled chords.
2. Singing an improvised melody while playing the harmonization.
3. Playing the chords in the left hand while improvising a melody in the right hand.
4. Transposing to C Major and G Major.

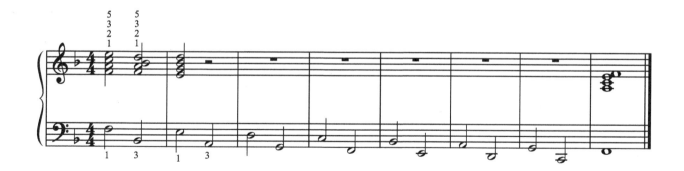

Practice Tips

✓ Practice transposing all exercises in this review to major and minor keys up to four flats and four sharps.

✓ Focus on using familiar patterns (triads in root position, arpeggios, and scales) and vary those patterns by rolling chords, adding nonchord tones, and using different registers.

✓ Use a metronome to keep a steady beat.

✓ Use one predominant rhythmic pattern, such as triplets, dotted rhythms, or simple quarter- and half-note patterns, to give your improvisation structural unity.

✓ Feature only one type of nonchord tone at first then gradually add more.

✓ Practice playing familiar songs in opposite characters: change major to minor; use fast tempos instead of slower ones; and play in contrasting registers of the keyboard.

✓ Experiment with playing in different styles (for example, a jazz version of "Mary Had a Little Lamb").

✓ Vary the accompaniment patterns. Use the lefthand examples in Review V as a basis for varying the patterns.

✓ Be careful with melodic structure: Use clear question-and-answer phrasing (antecedent and consequent) with traditional harmonic progressions.

✓ Listen for clean pedal changes.

Review VIII

Score Reading

The score-reading examples in this review include excerpts from band, orchestral, choral, and string quartet repertoire. Score reading presents several challenges to the emerging pianist, as it requires visually separating the parts, reading different clefs simultaneously, and often transposing instruments to concert pitch. Highlighting the parts, identifying familiar patterns in the melodic movement, and writing in harmonic analysis are all helpful ways to build score-reading abilities.

Practice Tips

✓ Read from the lowest staff up, keeping your eyes on the page as much as possible.

✓ When transposing to concert pitch, remember the adage: "An instrument sees a C and sounds its key." For example, the B♭ clarinet sees a C on the staff, but sounds a B♭. Therefore, for concert pitch you read a C on the staff but play a B♭ on the piano.

✓ For B♭ transposition, read a whole step below the note on the staff.

✓ For E♭ transposition, read in bass clef, but be careful to play in the correct octave for the instrument on the piano.

✓ For F transposition, read in bass clef, but up a whole step from the written note, being careful to play in the correct octave for the instrument on the piano.

✓ Remember to transpose the key by the same interval as the key of the transposing instrument is from C. For example, the E♭ alto saxophone sounds a Major 6th below C. If the E♭ alto saxophone melody is in the key of F Major, a Major 6th below F is A♭. Therefore the key of the work is A♭ Major.

✓ For traditional works, always check a nontransposing instrument to make sure you have transposed to the correct key.

✓ For C clefs, remember that the designated line of the clef sign is Middle C on the piano. If you have difficulty reading in C clef, the intervals can be related to treble clef:

• For alto clef, read in treble clef but a step above each note, being careful of the key signature and other accidentals.

• For tenor clef, read in treble clef but a step below each note, being careful of the key signature and other accidentals.

✓ Play two parts simultaneously, with one nontransposing instrument in one hand and a transposing instrument in the other (i.e., right hand plays the flute line and left hand plays the B♭ clarinet line).

✓ Practice reading different combinations of lines together, including adjacent lines and lines that are far apart.

✓ For choral scores, practice single lines and playing two, three, and four parts simultaneously.

Score-Reading Excerpts

Excerpt from *Ave Verum Corpus*, K. 618

W. A. Mozart (1756–1791)

104

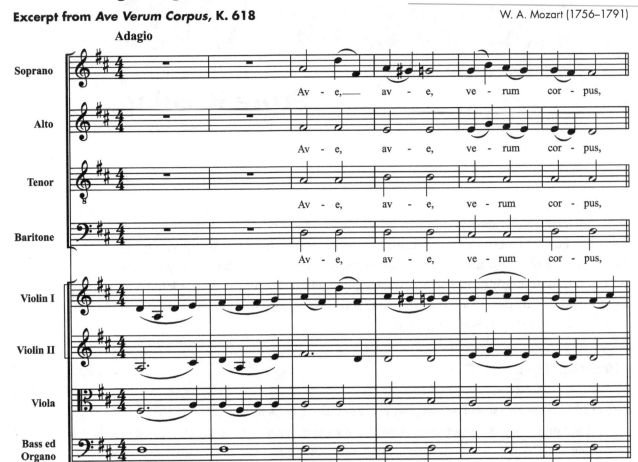

Excerpt from *Liebeslieder Waltzes,* Op. 52, No .1

Johannes Brahms (1833–1897)

Excerpt from "Ach Gott und Herr," BWV 48

Anon./arr. J. S. Bach (1685–1750)

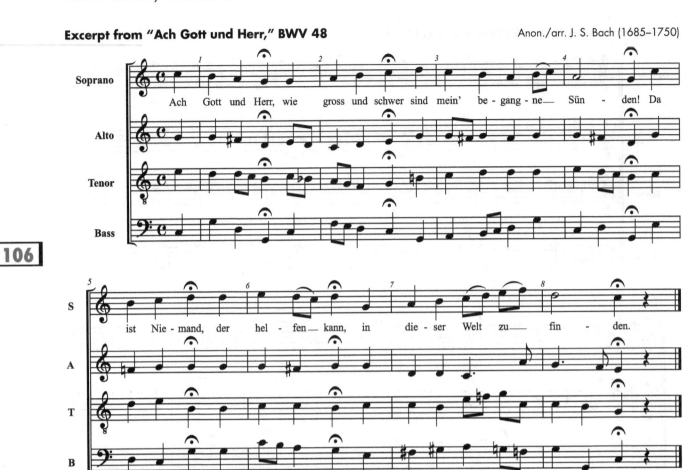

106

Excerpt from "Vater unser im Himmelreich," BWV 416

Anon./arr. J. S. Bach (1685–1750)

Va - ter un - ser im Him - mel - reich, der du uns al - le hei - ssest gleich Brü -

der sein — und dich ru - fen an und willst das Be - ten von uns ha'n, gib,

dass nicht bet' al - lein der Mund, hilf, dass es — geh' von Her - zens Grund.

Excerpt from *Messiah*, HWV 56

George Frideric Handel (1685–1759)

Soprano: Hal - le - lu - jah! Hal - le - lu - jah! Hal - le - lu - jah! Hal - le - lu - jah! Hal -

Alto: Hal - le - lu - jah! Hal - le - lu - jah! Hal - le - lu - jah! Hal - le - lu - jah! Hal -

Tenor: Hal - le - lu - jah! Hal - le - lu - jah! Hal - le - lu - jah! Hal - le - lu - jah! Hal -

Bass: Hal - le_____ Hal - le - lu - jah! Hal - le - lu - jah! Hal - le - lu - jah! Hal -

S: le - lu - jah! Hal - le - lu - jah! Hal - le - lu - jah! Hal - le - lu - jah! Ha - le - lu - jah! Ha -

A: le - lu - jah! Hal - le - lu - jah! Hal - le - lu - jah! Hal - le - lu - jah! Ha - le - lu - jah! Ha -

T: le - lu - jah! Hal - le - lu - jah! Hal - le - lu - jah! Hal - le - lu - jah! Ha - le - lu - jah! Ha -

B: le - lu - jah! Hal - le - lu - jah! Hal - le - lu - jah! Hal - le - lu - jah! Ha - le - lu - jah! Ha -

S: le_____ lu - jah! for the Lord God Om - ni - po - tent reign - eth.

A: le lu - jah! for the Lord God Om - ni - po - tent reign - eth.

T: le_____ lu - jah! for the Lord God Om - ni - po - tent reign - eth.

B: le_____ lu - jah! for the Lord God Om - ni - po - tent reign - eth.

Excerpt from *Messiah*, HWV 56

George Frideric Handel (1685–1759)

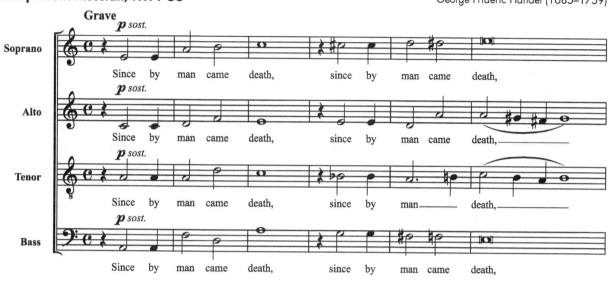

Excerpt from "Es ist ein' Ros' enstprungen"

Michael Praetorius (1571–1621)

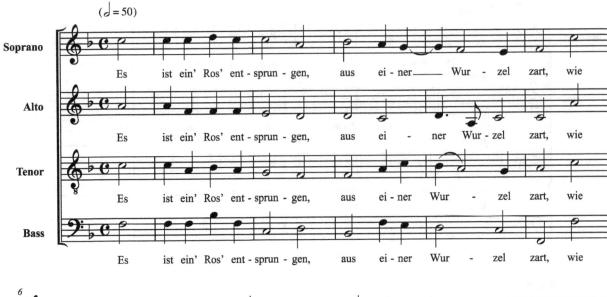

110

Excerpt from "Schöne Fremde"

Fanny Hensel (1805–1847)

Rund._____ es rau - schen die Wi - pfel, als hiel - ten zu die - ser

Rund._____ es rau - schen die Wi - pfel, als hiel - ten zu die - ser

Rund._____ es rau - schen die Wi - pfel, als hiel - ten zu die - ser

Rund._____ es rau - schen die Wi - pfel, als hiel - ten zu die - ser

Stund,_____ die al - ten, al - ten Göt - ter die Rund._____

Stund,_____ die al - ten, al - ten Göt - ter die Rund._____

Stund,_____ die al - ten, al - ten Göt - ter die Rund._____

Stund,_____ die al - ten, al - ten Göt - ter die Rund._____

Excerpt from "Oh! weep for those"

Maurice Arnold (1865–1937)

Excerpt from *Marienlieder,* Op. 22, No. 1

Johannes Brahms (1833–1897)

Con moto

Sopran

f

1. Ge - grü - ßet Ma - ri - a, du Mut - ter der
2. Ma - ri - a, du sollst ei - nen Sohn___ emp -

Alto

f

1. Ge - grü - ßet, ge - grü - ßet___ Ma - ri - a, du Mut - ter der
2. Ma - ri - a, Ma - ri - a,___ du sollst ei - nen Sohn___ emp -

Tenor

f

1. Ge - grü - ßet, ge - grü - ßet Ma - ri - a,___ du Mut - ter der
2. Ma - ri - a, Ma - ri - a,___ du sollst ei - nen Sohn___ emp -

Baß

f

1. Ma - ri - a,___ du Mut - ter der
2. Du sollst ei - nen Sohn___ emp -

S

f

Gna - den! Ge - grü - ßet Ma - ri - a, du Mut - ter der Gna - den!
fan - gen! Ma - ri - a, du sollst ei - nen Sohn___ emp - fan - gen!

A

f

Gna - den! Ge - grü - ßet, ge - grü - ßet Ma - ri - a, du Mut - ter der Gna - den!
fan - gen! Ma - ri - a, Ma - ri - a,___ du sollst ei - nen Sohn___ emp - fan - gen!

T

f

Gna - den! Ge - grü - ßet, ge - grü - ßet Ma - ri - a,___ du Mut - ter der Gna - den!
fan - gen! Ma - ri - a, Ma - ri - a,___ du sollst ei - nen Sohn___ emp - fan - gen!

B

f

Gna - den! Ma - ri - a,___ du Mut - ter der Gna - den!
fan - gen! du sollst ei - nen Sohn___ emp - fan - gen!

114

Excerpt from *A German Requiem*, Op. 45

Johannes Brahms (1833–1897)

Excerpt from String Quartet, K. 157, Mvt. 1

W. A. Mozart (1756–1791)

117

118

O Tannenbaum

Traditional/arr. Scott Beard (b. 1964)

119

Excerpt from St. Anthony Chorale, Hob. II/46

Joseph Haydn (1732–1809)

Excerpt from *Second Suite in F for Military Band,* Op. 28, No. 2

Gustav Holst (1874–1934)

Review IX

Solo Repertoire

Performing a solo piece is one of the most enjoyable and important ways to demonstrate your piano proficiency. The solo works in this review are based on many of the keyboard patterns you have been studying.

Practice Tips

✓ Check your seating position. Stay in one place on the bench and lean to the right or left for passages in higher or lower registers.

✓ Follow all fingerings.

✓ Analyze the music, marking patterns, harmonic movement, and structure.

✓ Observe and listen for all dynamics and articulations. Generally, unless otherwise marked, use good legato being careful not to overlap the fingers.

✓ Practice broken chords as solid chords, with the fingerings marked in the score.

✓ Check the tempo marking and use a metronome to work up to the suggested tempo.

✓ Think about how the title relates to the piece. Use the Glossary for additional information.

✓ For pieces with pedal, have your foot in place on the pedal from the beginning of the piece. Use the damper pedal sparingly, being careful to pedal cleanly (changing frequently with the harmonic and melodic lines) and keeping the heel of your right foot on the floor.

Practice Tips—Allegro from Sonatina, Op. 36, No. 1

✓ Suggested tempo: ♩ = 68–72.

✓ Practice slowly using a quarter note beat on the metronome. Work up to a pulse of 2 beats per measure.

✓ Use a legato touch throughout, observing the contrasting two-note and other slur articulations.

✓ Listen for balance between the melody and the accompaniment and dynamic changes.

Muzio Clementi was a highly successful composer, teacher, music publisher, and piano manufacturer. Clementi was known for having an outstanding piano technique. His Sonatinas, Op. 36, are a staple of the early-grade piano repertoire.

The markings show the type of analysis you should prepare for each of the solo works studied in this review. The keys and the structure are labeled and brackets outline triads in root, first, and second inversions as well as scales and five-finger patterns.

First movement from Sonatina, Op. 36, No. 1

Muzio Clementi (1752–1832)

125

Practice Tips—Musette in D Major, BWV Anh. 126

✓ Suggested tempo: ♩ = 72–80.

✓ Notice the five-finger patterns and broken triads throughout.

✓ On the repeats, experiment with dynamic changes.

A *musette* is a dance from the seventeenth and early eighteenth centuries inspired by a type of bagpipe instrument of the same name. Written for Bach's wife Anna Magdalena, this musette features a broken-octave bass accompaniment as well as sections written in unison between the hands. The work has a simple ABA form.

127

Musette in D Major, BWV Anh.126

Johann Sebastian Bach (1685–1750)

(Allegretto)

Practice Tips—Arabesque, Op. 100, No. 2

✓ Suggested tempo: ♩ = 90–112.
✓ Continue the staccato in the introductory lefthand chords throughout the piece.
✓ Notice the familiar five-finger patterns and the lefthand chords based on cadence patterns throughout.
✓ Keep the last note of the slur light as you lift for the phrase end.

German pianist and composer Johann Friedrich Burgmüller wrote numerous collections of pedagogical works for beginning and intermediate students. His *25 Easy and Progressive Studies*, Op. 100, contains many staples of the beginning repertoire. An *arabesque* is a type of nineteenth-century character piece for the piano that is usually in ternary (ABA) form and features ornamental themes or flourishes.

129

Arabesque, Op. 100, No. 2

Johann Friedrich Burgmüller (1806–1874)

Practice Tips—Écossaise, WoO 23

✓ Suggested tempo: ♩ = 72–80.

✓ Mark the chord patterns in the A section and the triadic outlines of the lefthand octaves in the B section.

✓ Experiment with dynamic changes on the repeats.

Although Beethoven is known more as a composer of large-scale works, he did write several accessible pieces for the beginning pianist. An *écossaise* is a country dance in duple meter, most likely of Scottish origin. In binary form, the B section here begins by emphasizing the dominant before cadencing on the final G-Major tonic chord.

Écossaise in G Major, WoO 23

Ludwig van Beethoven (1770–1827)

131

Practice Tips—Allegro from Sonatina in G Major

✓ Suggested tempo: ♩ = 104–126.
✓ Mark the familiar five-finger patterns, scales, and triadic outlines.
✓ Use a legato touch throughout.
✓ Listen for balance between the melody and accompaniment.

English composer Thomas Attwood was a student of Mozart. He became a musician in service to the King of England. This first movement is from one of his best-known early piano sonatinas.

First movement from Sonatina in G Major

Thomas Attwood (1765–1838)

132

*The grace note can be played almost simultaneously with the main note.

Practice Tips—Prelude

✓ Suggested minimum tempo: ♩ = 60–63.

✓ Work up to the suggested tempo using a quarter-note beat.

✓ Bertini indicates alternating fingers in measures 9 through 16. If necessary, the fingering at the beginning of each pattern may be used throughout instead of the alternations. An additional fingering option is given in parentheses.

Henri Bertini was a French pianist, composer, and teacher. He was known for his elegance and high artistic standards, both in his performances and in his compositions. This prelude develops dexterity in the right hand and requires even attacks and good legato.

Prelude from *12 Short Pieces*   Henri Bertini (1798–1876)

134

Practice Tips—Moderato from Sonatina in G Major

✓ Suggested tempo: ♩ = 92–100.
✓ Notice the five-finger patterns, scales, and triadic outlines.
✓ Use a legato touch throughout in both hands.
✓ Listen for balance between the melody and accompaniment.

The first movement of this Sonatina in G follows a similar path as the previous sonatina by Attwood, however Beethoven includes a coda beginning in measure 25. The two-note slurs require a slight separation, with the second note softer than the first.

First movement from Sonatina in G Major

Ludwig van Beethoven (1770–1827)

*The grace note can be played almost simultaneously with the main note.

Practice Tips—Rondo

✓ Suggested tempo: ♩. = 72–80.
✓ Play the grace notes almost simultaneously with the main note.
✓ Mark the familiar chordal patterns throughout.
✓ Practice the left hand as blocked chords.

Bertini wrote more than five hundred studies for the piano. A *rondo* is a musical form that features a main theme that returns several times, juxtaposed with contrasting melodies. Here Bertini combines elements of rondo and ABA form.

Rondo from *12 Short Pieces*

Henri Bertini (1798–1876)

138

Da capo sin' al Fine

139

Practice Tips—Rondoletto, Op. 60, No. 3

✓ Suggested tempo: ♩ = 108.
✓ Be careful to follow all fingerings.
✓ Listen for dynamic differences and articulation.

Margaret Ruthven Lang has the distinction of being the first female composer to have a work performed by a major American orchestra. Her compositions include numerous songs as well as choral and solo piano works. A *rondoletto* is a brief rondo.

Rondoletto from *Three Pieces for Young Players*, Op. 60

Margaret Ruthven Lang (1867–1972)

141

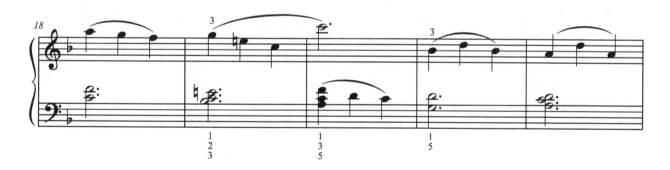

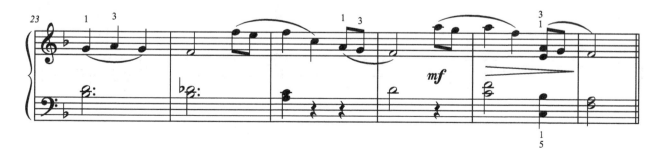

Practice Tips—Rhapsody in E Minor

✓ Suggested tempo: ♩ = 116–120.
✓ Use good legato throughout.
✓ Listen for the dynamic differences.
✓ Listen for clean pedal changes.
✓ Stay in one place on the bench and lean to the upper and lower registers as needed.

A *rhapsody* is a one-movement work popular in the Romantic era that was meant to portray a range of emotions with contrasting themes and a broad use of the piano. This rhapsody makes dramatic use of hand-over-hand arpeggios, harmonic minor scales, and alternating triads.

Rhapsody in E Minor

Scott Beard (b. 1964)

145

147

Practice Tips—The Orphan, Op. 64, No. 4

✓ Suggested tempo: ♩. = 54–63.
✓ Practice the lefthand broken chords as blocked chords.
✓ Use good legato throughout in both hands.
✓ Use the pedal throughout. Be careful to release for the rests and change for the step-wise melodic notes.
✓ Play the grace notes almost simultaneously with the main note.

Louis Streabbog was the pseudonym of Belgian pianist Jean Louis Gobbaerts. He was a prolific composer of piano works and today is known for his many pedagogical pieces. *The Orphan* is in ternary (ABA) form. The middle section modulates to the relative major before returning to the opening material and key in measure 36.

The Orphan, Op. 64, No. 4

Louis Streabbog (1835–1886)

149

Practice Tips—Autumn Mist

✓ Suggested tempo: ♩ = 88–96.

✓ Use pedal and good legato throughout. Pedal once per measure.

✓ Measure 20 employs the use of a "finger" pedal, requiring the performer to hold the lowest note while continuing the pattern.

Autumn Mist is based on recurring melodic, rhythmic, and harmonic patterns. The opening five measures can be played freely with a bell-like sound. The ending should sound exotic, with the unexpected A-Major harmony. Let the music gradually fade away for an effective ending.

Autumn Mist

Scott Beard (b. 1964)

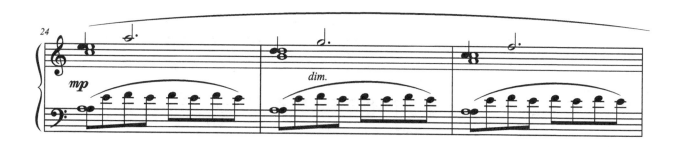

Practice Tips—Prelude, Op. 28, No. 4

✓ Suggested tempo: ♩ = 60–72.
✓ The chordal patterns here change in a very subtle manner. Look for common tones to help guide the hand as the chords change.
✓ Use a "shallow" pedal, depressing lightly.

One of the most famous and accessible of Chopin's preludes, this work requires careful attention to balance and coordination of the more complicated harmonic changes. The constant eighth-note rhythm of the left hand acts as a kind of ostinato.

Prelude in E Minor, Op. 28, No. 4

Frédéric Chopin (1810–1849)

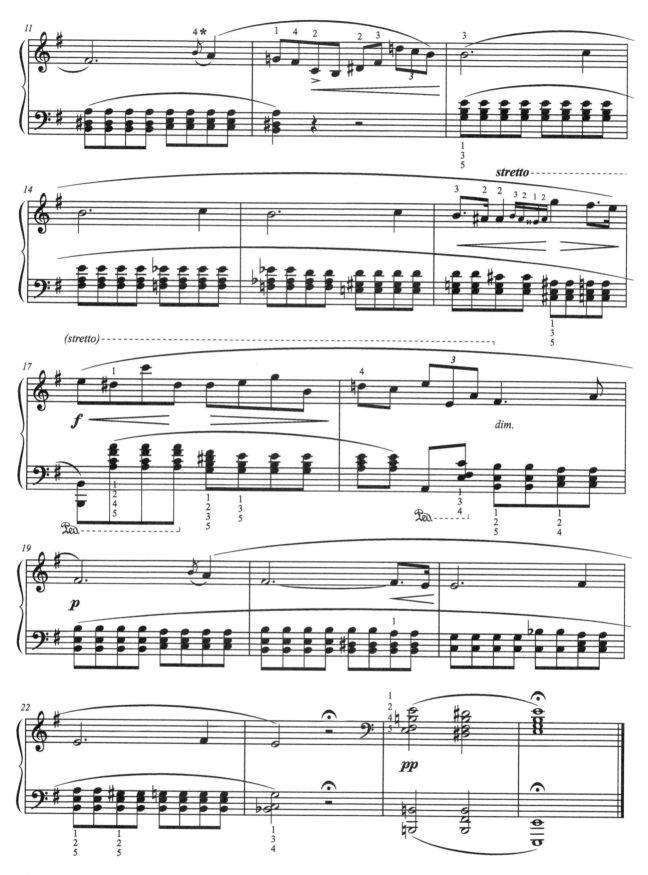

*The grace note can be played on the beat slightly before the main note.

Review X

Practice Exams

This review contains four practice piano proficiency exams. Record yourself as you take each exam and use the rubric below to help assess your work. Each exam area is worth 10 points. A passing score is 70 points or more out of 100.

Evaluation Rubric					
	Poor .5 point	Fair 1 point	Good 1.5 points	Very Good 2 points	Excellent 2.5 points
Posture: Seating position; finger, hand, arm placement	Poor seating and body positions	Minimal slouches, uncomfortable	Posture acceptable, technique acceptable	Very good posture, very good finger technique/ hand placement, minor problems with technique	Excellent posture, finger, hand and arm placement
Accuracy: Notes, fingering, articulation, pedaling	Major mistakes; poor performance	Some mistakes; poor recovery	Some mistakes; slow recovery; good effort	Minimal mistakes made with quick recovery	Very minimal mistakes; clear and accurate
Tempo/ Rhythm: Appropriate tempo, correct rhythm	Incorrect rhythm, tempo inappropriate and unsteady	Several rhythmic errors	Average rhythm and tempo	Good rhythm and tempo; few errors	Excellent rhythm and tempo
Dynamics/ Expression: Musical markings, character	Ignored all or most of the expression marks	Realized minimal expression marks	Basic sense of expression and dynamics	Realizes most dynamics and expressive marks	Very expressive, correct use of dynamics

Exam 1

1. Describe good seating and hand positions at the piano.

2. Scales: Play the following scales, two octaves, ascending and descending, hands together. The minimum tempo is ♩ = 80.

   F Major
   B Major
   C Harmonic Minor

3. Arpeggios: Play the following arpeggios, hands separately, two octaves, ascending and descending:

   G Major
   D Minor
   G♭ Major

4. Cadences: Play cadences, hands together, in root position, first inversion and second inversion, in the following keys:

   G Minor
   A♭ Major
   E Major

5. Vocal Warm-Ups: Sing and play one vocal warm-up in major, starting on D and moving up chromatically for six keys.

6. Harmonization and Transposition: Play "Happy Birthday" in G Major and transpose to C Major:

Hap - py birth - day to you, Hap - py birth - day to

you, Hap - py birth - day dear Hap - py birth - day to you.

7. Improvisation: Improvise on the first phrase of "Happy Birthday" with one added element of your choice in the key of your choice.

8. Sight Reading: Play the following example.

9. Score Reading: Play the Violin I, Violin II, and Viola lines simultaneously.

161

10. Solo Repertoire: Play your solo piece within the tempo range listed in the score.

Exam 2

1. Describe proper use of the damper pedal.

2. Scales: Play the following scales, two octaves, ascending and descending, hands together. The minimum tempo is ♩ = 80.

   D♭ Major
   E Harmonic Minor
   A Harmonic Minor

3. Arpeggios: Play arpeggios, hand over hand, six octaves, ascending and descending, in the following keys.

   A♭ Major
   E Major
   F Minor

4. Cadences: Play cadences, hands together, in first and second inversions, in the following keys:

   F Major
   B Major
   C Minor

5. Vocal Warm-Ups: Sing and play one vocal warm-up in minor, starting on A and moving up chromatically for four keys.

6. Harmonization and Transposition: Play "Go Tell It on the Mountain" in G Major and transpose to F Major:

7. Improvisation: Improvise on the first phrase of "Go Tell It on the Mountain" with one added element of your choice in G Major.

8. Sight Reading: Play the following example.

9. Score Reading: Play the tenor and bass lines simultaneously.

10. Solo Repertoire: Play your solo piece within the tempo range listed in the score.

Exam 3

1. Discuss the title of your solo piece. How does it relate to the music?

2. Scales: Play the following scales, two octaves, ascending and descending, hands together. The minimum tempo is ♩ = 80.

   F Harmonic Minor
   G Major
   B♭ Major

3. Arpeggios: Play arpeggios, hands together, two octaves, ascending and descending, in the following keys:

   D Major
   C Minor
   D♭ Major

4. Cadences: Play cadences in root position, first inversion and second inversion, in the following keys:

   G♭ Major
   E Minor
   B♭ Major

5. Vocal Warm-Ups: Sing and play one vocal warm-up in major, starting on F and moving up chromatically for five keys.

6. Harmonization and Transposition: Play "Auld Lang Syne" in F Major and transpose to G Major:

7. Improvisation: Improvise on the first phrase of "Auld Lang Syne" with an introduction and one element of your choice in F Major.

8. Sight Reading: Play the following example.

9. Score Reading: Play the flute and B♭ clarinet lines simultaneously.

10. Solo Repertoire: Play your solo piece within the tempo range listed in the score.

Exam 4

1. Discuss how you approach sight reading. What steps do you take to sight read successfully?

2. Scales: Play the following scales, two octaves, ascending and descending, hands together. The minimum tempo is ♩ = 80.

   G♭ Major
   E♭ Major
   F♯ Harmonic Minor

3. Arpeggios: Play arpeggios, hand-over-hand, six octaves, ascending and descending, in the following keys:

   B♭ Major
   B Minor
   G♯ Minor

4. Cadences: Play cadences in root position, first inversion and second inversion, in the following keys:

   B Minor
   D♭ Major
   A Major

5. Vocal Warm-Ups: Sing and play one vocal warm-up in minor, starting on C and moving up chromatically for six keys.

6. Harmonization and Transposition: Play "Greensleeves" in E Minor and transpose to D Minor:

7. Improvisation: Improvise on the first phrase of "Greensleeves" with two added elements of your choice.

8. Sight reading: Play the following example.

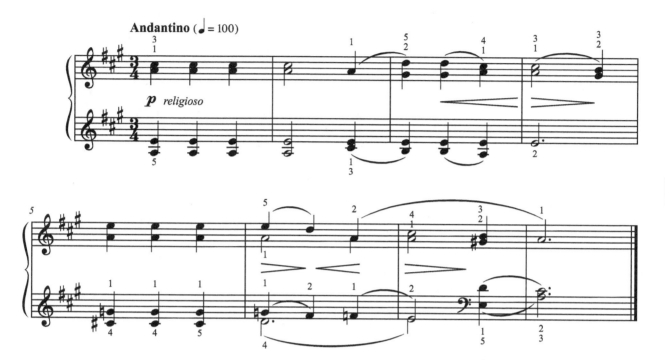

9. Score Reading: Play the soprano and bass lines simultaneously.

10. Solo Repertoire: Play your solo piece within the tempo range listed in the score.

APPENDIX I SUPPLEMENTAL SCALES, CHORDS, AND ARPEGGIOS

The scales, chords, and arpeggios are presented in the parallel keys. Some tonalities are written using enharmonic keys for ease in reading.

C Major

C Natural Minor

C Melodic Minor

C Harmonic Minor

G Major

G Natural Minor

G Melodic Minor

G Harmonic Minor

172

D Major

D Natural Minor

D Melodic Minor

D Harmonic Minor

A Major

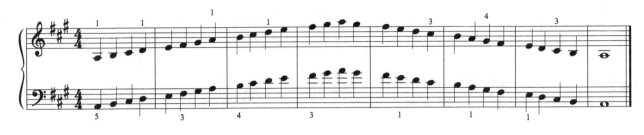

A Natural Minor

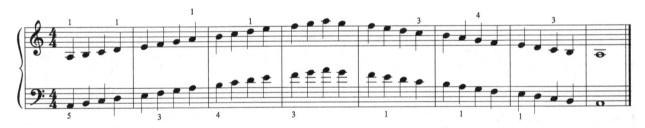

A Melodic Minor

A Harmonic Minor

E Major

E Natural Minor

E Melodic Minor

E Harmonic Minor

B Major

B Natural Minor

B Melodic Minor

B Harmonic Minor

G♭ Major (F♯ Major)

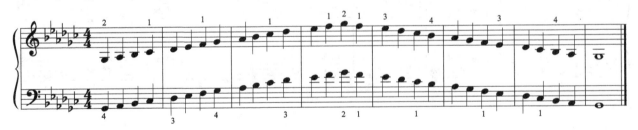

F# Natural Minor

F# Melodic Minor

F# Harmonic Minor

D♭ Major (C♯ Major)

C♯ Natural Minor

C♯ Melodic Minor

C♯ Harmonic Minor

A♭ Major

G♯ Natural Minor

G♯ Melodic Minor

G♯ Harmonic Minor

E♭ Major

Eb Natural Minor

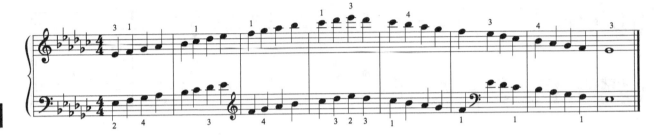

Eb Melodic Minor

Eb Harmonic Minor

B♭ Major

B♭ Natural Minor

B♭ Melodic Minor

B♭ Harmonic Minor

F Major

187

F Natural Minor

F Melodic Minor

F Harmonic Minor

188

APPENDIX II DIAGRAM OF THE PIANO

Grand Piano Exterior

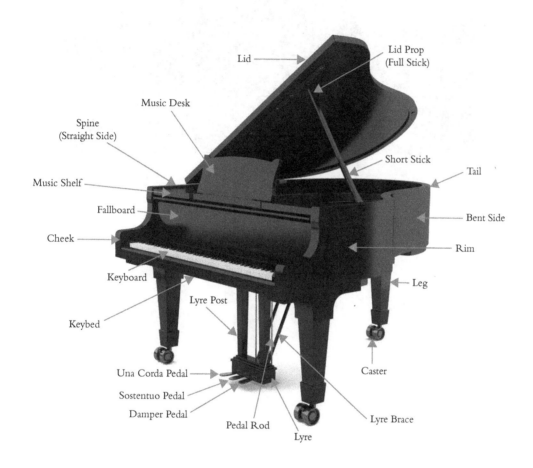

Lid

Lid Prop (Full Stick)

Music Desk

Spine (Straight Side)

Short Stick

Tail

Music Shelf

Fallboard

Bent Side

Cheek

Rim

Keyboard

Leg

Lyre Post

Keybed

Una Corda Pedal

Sostentuo Pedal

Damper Pedal

Pedal Rod

Lyre

Lyre Brace

Caster

Grand Piano Interior

APPENDIX III SELECTED COMPOSER BIOGRAPHIES

Thomas Attwood (1765–1838): English organist and composer Thomas Attwood was a student of Mozart. He served as the organist for St. Paul's Cathedral in London and also music instructor to English nobility. Attwood is best known for his anthems and pedagogical keyboard works, but he also composed music for plays and comic operas as well as part songs known as *glees*.

Maurice Arnold (1865–1937): Born Maurice Arnold Strothotte in Missouri, Arnold began piano lessons with his mother and later studied in Cincinnati and in Germany. He also worked with Dvořák during his time in America. Arnold's compositions include choral and orchestral works, two comic operas, and several pieces for solo piano and piano ensemble.

Johann Sebastian Bach (1685–1750): Bach's music represents the high point of the Baroque era and the contrapuntal style. Both his sacred and secular compositions have stood the test of time and are revered not only for their musical complexity but also for their beauty and depth of expression. He composed a great variety of keyboard pieces including two volumes of *The Well-Tempered Clavier*, suites, and toccatas.

Béla Bartók (1881–1945): Hungarian pianist Béla Bartók is regarded as one of the most important composers of the modern era. His analysis and cataloging of Eastern European folk music informs much of his piano writing, especially in works such as the *Mikrokosmos, Dances in Bulgarian Rhythm, Romanian Folk Dances,* and *Romanian Christmas Carols.*

Scott Beard (b. 1964): Pianist, teacher, administrator, and pedagogical composer, Beard was named 2006 West Virginia Music Teacher of the Year. His students have won prizes in state, regional, national, and international competitions and have gone on to study music at conservatories and major university music schools. He has performed as a soloist, chamber musician, and orchestral soloist throughout the United States, Europe, and South America.

Ludwig van Beethoven (1770–1827): Credited with bridging the Classical and Romantic eras, Beethoven is one of the most influential composers of all time. Beethoven considered himself a *Tondichter* (tone poet). He expanded traditional forms, increased technical demands, and explored new expressive possibilities. Beethoven's piano works span his entire compositional career with pieces at all levels of study.

Vincenzo Bellini (1801–1835): Bellini is known today for his landmark *bel canto* operas that feature long, flowing, and at times highly ornamented melodic lines. His music is said to have influenced Chopin. Bellini died at age 33, and almost all of his operas remain in the repertoire today, including *Norma, La Sonnambula*, and *I Puritani*.

Henri Bertini (1798–1876): Bertini was a French composer, pianist, and teacher. He was a child prodigy who performed as a soloist and as a member of chamber groups. He wrote more than five hundred piano etudes at various levels, usually grouped into collections of twenty-five pieces. Of note are his many studies for the left hand alone and for piano duet.

Nadia Boulanger (1887–1979): Boulanger is remembered today as one of the most influential teachers of the twentieth century. Her students included Aaron Copland, Quincy Jones, Phillip Glass, and Ned Rorem. She was an organist and pianist and dedicated much of her life to preserving the compositions of her sister Lili Boulanger, who died in 1918. As a composer, Nadia Boulanger's works include songs, a piano concerto, and pieces for piano, cello, and organ.

J. Friedrich Burgmüller (1806–1874): Burgmüller was a German pianist and composer. He moved to Paris in his late twenties and began to perform and compose in a salon style. Burgmüller is best known for his collections of character pieces and studies for piano, especially the *25 Études faciles et progressives*, Op. 100.

Frédéric Chopin (1810–1849): Chopin was born in Poland but spent much of his adult life in France. An innovative pianist and composer, his piano music has had unparalleled popularity. Chopin combined the influence of Polish folk music with a unique chromatic language and keyboard style, all of which make his music instantly recognizable. His earliest compositions and several of his *Preludes* are accessible to emerging pianists.

Muzio Clementi (1752–1832): Clementi was celebrated in his lifetime as a pianist, composer, music publisher, and piano manufacturer. Born in Italy, he moved to England as a teenager to advance his studies and remained there as he established his career. Today, Clementi is best known for his piano sonatas, sonatinas, and his method book, *Introduction to the Art of Playing the Pianoforte.*

P. A. Corri (1784–1832): Born in Edinburgh of Italian heritage (the son of composer Domenico Corri), Philip Antony Corri was an organist, pianist, composer, and pedagogue. In 1817, he moved to America and settled in Baltimore where he continued his musical career under the pseudonym Arthur Clifton. Corri wrote method books and composed a variety of instrumental works, including numerous piano pieces.

Carl Czerny (1791–1857): Czerny was an Austrian pianist, composer, and teacher and one of Beethoven's most famous pupils. His many collections of piano studies, over one thousand, are still widely used today. Notably, Czerny also wrote many pedagogical and concert works for piano duet, two pianos, six hands, and larger piano ensembles.

R. Nathaniel Dett (1882–1943): Nathaniel Dett had a multifaceted career as a music professor, composer, organist, and concert pianist. Dett studied at the Oberlin Conservatory of Music and also studied with Nadia Boulanger. He was influenced by Antonin Dvořák (1841–1904) and his use of folk elements. Dett is perhaps best known for his expertise in combining the Romantic style with elements of the African-American spiritual.

Stephen Foster (1826–1864): Born in Pennsylvania, Foster is considered America's first professional songwriter. He taught himself to play several instruments including the clarinet, violin, guitar, and piano. Many of his most famous songs were inspired by the places and people he knew, including "Camptown Races," "Tioga Waltz," and most notably "Jeanie with the Light Brown Hair," written for his wife Jane Denny McDowell.

Fanny Hensel (1805–1847): Born Fanny Mendelssohn, Hensel was a German pianist and composer and the sister of Felix Mendelssohn. An accomplished pianist, she began piano studies with her mother, whose teacher was a student of Bach. Hensel composed more than four hundred works including songs, piano pieces, and chamber works.

Louis Köhler (1820–1886): Köhler was a German composer, conductor, and piano teacher. In the 1850s he began to focus solely on teaching the piano and writing many of his now well-known pedagogical works. These include *12 Easy Studies*, Op. 157, *The Little Pianist*, Op. 189, and the *Short School of Velocity*, Op. 242.

Margaret Ruthven Lang (1867–1972): With her *Dramatic Overture* premiere in Boston in 1893, Lang was the first American female composer to have a work performed by a major American orchestra. She studied in Boston and Munich and knew many of the great artists of her time, including Liszt, Wagner, Dvořák, and Paderewski. She is perhaps best known for her more than two hundred songs, which have been performed internationally.

Hélène Liebmann (1796—after 1835): Liebmann was a child prodigy, both as a composer and as a pianist, in her native Germany. She composed chamber music and pieces for piano, dedicating most of her works to her teacher Ferdinand Ries (1784–1838), who studied with Beethoven. The exact date of her death is not known. The last known mention of her is in Clara Wieck's diary, which states that Liebmann was present at her concert in 1835.

Leopold Mozart (1719–1787): Known today primarily as the father of Wolfgang Amadeus Mozart and his sister Nannerl, Leopold Mozart was a respected composer, conductor, teacher, and violinist. He wrote symphonies, instrumental works, and pieces for his children's piano study, as well as the highly regarded *Treatise on the Fundamental Principles of Violin Playing*.

Giovanni Battista Pergolesi (1710–1736): An Italian composer, organist, and violinist, Pergolesi wrote *opera buffa* and chamber, keyboard, and orchestral works during his short life. He is best known for his sacred work *Stabat Mater* and the opera *La Serva Padrona*. His music reflects the appealing melodies and rhythmic vitality of the Italian Baroque style.

Jean-Philippe Rameau (1683–1764): Rameau was a leading French composer and harpsichordist and one of the most important music theorists of the Baroque era. He composed a number of successful operas, keyboard pieces, and choral and instrumental works. His *Treatise on Harmony* (1722) established his reputation and is a highly influential resource for music theory instruction.

Arnoldo Sartorio (1853–1936): Of Italian heritage, Sartorio was born in Germany and trained in the German music tradition as a composer, pianist, and teacher. Like Czerny, he was prolific in his output, with more than a thousand works. He wrote piano concertos, character pieces, and many collections of etudes for the developing pianist, as well as the *Sight Reading Exercises*, Op 45.

Franz Schubert (1797–1828): During his brief life, Schubert was a remarkably prolific composer. His works include symphonies, chamber works, operas, and numerous piano pieces. His music is imbued with Viennese folk songs and features a refined sense of harmony and expression. Schubert's greatest contribution is perhaps found in his more than six hundred Lieder, which essentially established the art song genre.

Clara Schumann (1819–1896): Clara Schumann was one of the leading pianists of the nineteenth century. Along with Franz Liszt, she established the tradition of performing piano recitals from memory. She championed the works of her husband Robert Schumann (1810–1856) and the music of Johannes Brahms (1833–1897). Most of her compositions were written prior to Robert's death and include works for piano solo, Lieder, and a piano concerto.

Louis Streabbog (1835–1886): Pseudonym of the Belgian pianist and composer Jean Louis Gobbaerts. He composed numerous works for the piano including character pieces and collections of etudes such as the well-known *12 Very Easy and Melodious Studies*, Op. 63, and the *12 Easy and Melodious Studies*, Op. 64.

Pauline Viardot (1821–1910): Viardot, of Spanish origin and the daughter of famed tenor, teacher, and impresario Manuel García, was a leading mezzo-soprano with a legacy as a pianist, pedagogue, and composer. She studied with Liszt, who thought highly of her playing. In addition to art songs, Viardot's compositions include operas and piano pieces.

GLOSSARY

Accent: A special emphasis on a note or chord. In piano playing, an accent is typically achieved by playing a louder sound within the context of the dynamics using a slightly faster attack on the key.

Accompaniment: Music that provides support or enhances a melody. In beginning-level solo piano works, the accompaniment is typically found in the left hand with the melody in the right hand. In advanced repertoire, the melody and accompaniment may occur within the same hand or between the hands. In ensemble works, the piano is the standard instrument to serve in an accompanying role.

Alla tedesca: Italian term meaning "in the style of a German dance."

Arabesque: A type of character piece, usually in ternary (ABA) form, that features ornate melodic figures or flourishes, similar to decorative scrollwork found in art and architecture. Friedrich Burgmüller (1806–1874), Robert Schumann (1810–1856), and Claude Debussy (1862–1918) composed some of the best known arabesques for piano.

Arpeggio: From the Italian *arpeggiare*, or "harp-like" playing. On the piano, the arpeggio is a broken chord played ascending or descending in one or both hands.

Art song: A composition for solo voice and piano accompaniment based on a poem or other literary text. Arts songs flourished in the nineteenth century in Germany beginning with Schubert, who composed more than six hundred songs known as *Lieder*. French art songs are commonly known as *mélodies*.

Articulation: In piano playing, articulation refers to the attack and release of the key along with the duration of the sound. The two most basic types of articulation are legato and staccato.

Authentic cadence: A chord progression at the end of a phrase or work that moves from the dominant (V) to the tonic (I or i). Based on the voicing, the authentic cadence may be categorized as perfect or imperfect.

Binary form: The structure of a composition that includes two sections (A and B) that are each typically repeated. The first section often modulates to a closely related key, such as the dominant or relative major. This was a popular form for keyboard music during the Baroque period. Johann Sebastian Bach composed many examples including short dances in the notebook written for his second wife, Anna Magdalena.

Burleske: A spirited musical work that combines comic and serious elements. An early example for keyboard, circa 1760, is by Mozart's father, Leopold Mozart (1719–1787).

Cadence: A chord progression. Cadences are often used as exercises for developing piano technique and are found in music typically at the conclusion of a phrase or work.

Character piece: Piano works popular in the Romantic era that were programmatic in nature and often had descriptive titles. Many of these were written in ternary (ABA) form.

Chorale: A vocal composition usually in four parts, with the melody in the top voice harmonized by the lower three. Beginning in the sixteenth century and synonymous with the Protestant hymn, the overarching texture of the chorale is homophonic with clear cadence points that punctuate the text. J. S. Bach used chorales as the basis for organ compositions, cantatas, and oratorios.

Chord: Three or more notes played simultaneously. In piano playing, chords are notated as vertically stacked pitches on the staff, Roman numerals, or as "pop" symbols found on lead sheets.

Chromatic scale: A scale entirely made up of half steps.

Damper pedal: The right pedal on the piano, which lifts the dampers and allows the sympathetic vibration of all the strings. The damper pedal adds color and sustains the sound.

Écossaise: A popular dance in the late 1700s and early 1800s characterized by a lively rhythm in duple meter and quick dynamic changes.

Etude: From the French *étudier* (to study). An etude typically focuses on developing a specific aspect of technique. As the piano gained popularity in the late eighteenth and early nineteenth centuries, numerous composers wrote collections of etudes for students, including Henri Bertini (1798–1876), J. F. Burgmüller (1806–1874), Carl Czerny (1791–1857), Stephen Heller (1813–1888), and Louis Köhler (1820–1886).

Fallboard: The keyboard cover on a piano.

Five-finger pattern: In piano study, the first five notes of a scale using all five fingers consecutively ascending and descending.

Form: The structure of a musical composition. Typical forms employed in piano music include binary, ternary, rondo, and sonata. The various sections within these forms provide contrast, or in some cases repetition, as the entire composition unfolds.

Half cadence: A progression that ends on the dominant (V). The half cadence sounds incomplete and is usually followed by another cadence that provides a stronger resolution.

Half step: The smallest standard musical interval. On the piano, the half step is from one key to the very next, also known as moving chromatically.

Harmonic minor scale: This scale uses the notes of the natural minor scale but with the 7th scale degree raised a half step. It is so named as the raised 7th alters the harmonies of the V and vii chords to major and diminished, respectively.

Harmonization: The accompaniment for a melodic line based on the harmony or chord progression outlined in the melody.

Harmony: Two or more notes played simultaneously.

Improvisation: The art of creating music "on the spot." Performers improvise by composing or varying a given musical motive without prior preparation, relying on known elements of harmonic, melodic, rhythmic, and formal structure.

Interval: The distance from one note (pitch) to another. Intervals are identified by quality and number as well as either harmonic or melodic. Intervals are the fundamental building blocks of musical composition.

Keybed: The large wood support underneath the keyboard on the piano.

Lead sheet: A melodic line on a single notated staff usually with words below and chord symbols above.

Legato: An Italian term that means "connected." Legato is at the foundation of piano playing. It is implied in most piano music or it may be indicated by a slur. Legato is achieved on the piano by connecting one note (finger) to the next, or as one finger presses down on the key, the other comes up, without any gap or overlap in the sound.

Lied: A type of art song originating in Germany, written for solo voice and piano accompaniment and based on a poem or other literary text.

Melodic minor scale: This scale uses the notes of the natural minor scale but with the 6th and 7th scale degrees raised a half-step ascending and lowered a half step descending. It is named after the practice of avoiding the augmented 2nd interval between the 6th and 7th degrees in an ascending minor melody by raising both pitches and in a descending melody by lowering the pitches to retain the minor sound.

Melody: One note performed at a time in an organized arrangement. Melody is typically the predominant feature of a composition.

Minuet (Menuet): A dance in triple meter. Originating in France, the minuet was especially popular in the seventeenth and eighteenth centuries.

Modulation: The process of moving from one key (tonality) to another. Modulation is an important element in delineating the structure of a composition.

Musette: A dance from the seventeenth and early eighteenth centuries inspired by a type of bagpipe instrument of the same name.

Musical era: A time period used to define particular characteristics and designate the major developments in Western music. The following standard eras are represented in the music throughout this book:
- *Baroque (1600–1750):* The height of the era is epitomized in the contrapuntal works of J. S. Bach (1685–1750) and G. F. Handel (1685–1759). The keyboard instruments included the harpsichord, clavichord, and organ, with the addition of the development of the piano in the early 1700s.
- *Classical (1750–1820):* The piano began its rise as the preeminent solo keyboard instrument. The sonata emerged as the characteristic form of the era, emphasizing contrasting melodies and dynamics.
- *Romantic (1820–1900):* The range and strength of the piano expanded, along with the rise of the virtuoso concert pianist. Composers highlighted the

197

increased expressive capabilities of the piano as well as an increasingly chromatic harmonic language.

- *20th Century* (1900–2000): A variety of musical styles emerged, including Impressionism, Expressionism, and Neo-Romanticism, all of which explored further expressive possibilities of the piano.
- *Contemporary* (2000–today): Today's piano compositions are informed by a variety of musical influences, with both traditional and nontraditional uses of the piano.

Natural minor scale: Also known as the "pure" minor, this scale is based on the key signature of the relative major and uses only the notes of the relative major scale.

Ostinato: A repeated musical motive, rhythm, or pattern.

Parallel key: Tonalities that share the same tonic such as C major and C minor.

Period: A type of melodic structure with an antecedent phrase that usually ends with a half cadence on the dominant (the question) followed by a consequent phrase that has a conclusive cadence (the answer). Both phrases typically begin with the same melodic material.

Phrase: A musical sentence. Phrases are usually combined in groups or periods, which form larger units within a composition.

Piano: Developed in 1700 by Bartolomeo Cristofori (1655–1731), an Italian musical instrument maker. Originally it was called the *Gravicembalo col piano e forte* (harpsichord with soft and loud). The name highlighted the instrument's ability to produce soft and loud sounds and eventually became shortened to the piano.

Piano action: The mechanical parts involved in striking the strings on a piano. A piano action may be described as "heavy" or "light" depending on the amount of depth or resistance the fingers feel when striking the keys.

Piano reduction: A condensed version of an instrumental or vocal score arranged for the piano. This allows the conductor or accompanist to play the score on the piano with ease.

Plagal cadence: A progression that moves from the subdominant (IV) to the tonic (I). It is sometimes known as the "Amen" cadence because of its use in closing standard hymns.

Pop symbol: Chord designations found in popular music. The capital letter represents the basic triad, the small case letter or abbreviation represents the quality, and the capital letter following the slash (/) denotes the note in the bass.

Portato: An articulation indicated by a dot combined with a slur or tenuto mark. Also known as mezzo-staccato, it is a slight separation between notes.

Prelude: The title *prelude* has been used for a variety of keyboard works since the early seventeenth century when it denoted an introductory piece. Chopin's *Preludes*, Op. 28, are credited with inspiring the use of the prelude as an independent character piece, typically centered on a single mood or image.

Preluding: The art of improvising a brief work before the performance of a solo piano work, a practice that was popular in the nineteenth century.

Relative key: Relative keys share the same key signature between the major and minor tonalities, such as C Major and A Minor. In a major scale, the name of the relative minor is the sixth note (submediant) of the scale. In a minor scale, the name of the relative major is the third note (mediant) of the scale.

Rhapsody: A one-movement work popular in the Romantic era meant to portray a range of emotions with contrasting themes and a broad use of the piano.

Rondo: A musical form that features a main theme that returns several times, juxtaposed with other themes that vary in character and often in key. A typical structure is ABACABA.

Scale: A set of pitches played in succession either ascending or descending and following a specific pattern of whole steps and half steps. On the piano, students play the traditional major and minor scales in multiple octaves in a variety of configurations between the hands.

Scale degree: The note (degree) of a scale relative to the distance from the first note (tonic). The scale-degree names, which are also denoted by Roman numerals (by capitals for major and small case for minor) for the triads built on them, are: Tonic (I, i); Supertonic (ii, ii°); Mediant (iii, III, III⁺); Subdominant (IV, iv); Dominant (V, v); Submediant (vi, VI); and Subtonic or Leading Tone (VII, vii°). The Subdominant and Submediant are so named because they are the dominant and mediant degrees below the tonic.

Score reading: Playing an instrumental or vocal score on the piano. This includes reading multiple lines and clefs simultaneously and also transposing to concert pitch.

Sight reading: Known as *prima vista* in Italian, the playing of a piece of music that the performer has not previously seen. The performer is expected to play the music as accurately as possible with a continuous flow of the rhythm.

Slur: A curved line that indicates both a phrase and, often in piano music, legato.

Sonatina: A "little sonata." Typically a multimovement work, smaller in scope and less demanding technically than the sonata, with the first movement based on sonata form. The name *sonata* comes from the Italian *sonare* (to play) and was first used as a general title for instrumental pieces in the seventeenth century.

Staccato: From the Italian word for separated or detached. Staccato is a type of articulation signified by a dot or wedge above or below the notehead. To create the separation between notes, the pianist must release the key. The wedge is typically the shortest staccato, followed by the dot and the dot with a slur or tenuto mark (portato).

Tenuto: A horizontal line indicating to hold the note or chord for its full value.

Ternary form: Also known as "song form." The structure of a musical composition that has three parts (ABA). The return of the "A" section repeats the opening material, but often with some variant that brings the piece to a close.

Texture: The lines or layers of writing in a musical composition. A work's complexity is often determined by its texture. In solo piano music, the texture may be contrapuntal (two or more melodic lines played simultaneously) or homophonic (melody with accompaniment). A monophonic texture is a single line of music.

Tie: A curved line between the same notes indicating to hold the pitch for the combined note values.

Tonic: The first degree of a scale, the tonal center or "home" key.

Two-note slur: A characteristic articulation and expressive gesture indicated by a slur between two different notes. In piano playing, this is achieved with a slight "down-up" motion of the wrist, with the stronger first note connected to the second note, which is detached or lifted softly.

Una corda: Italian for "one string." The left or "soft" pedal on the piano. This pedal moves the keyboard, which allows the hammers to strike fewer strings with a fuller part of the felt. It is often indicated as "u.c."

Whole step: Two half steps combined. Along with half step, the primary designation for measuring intervallic distance in music.

INDEX